big & SMALL

Original Korean text and illustrations by Dreaming Tortoise
Korean edition © Aram Publishing

This English edition published by big & SMALL in 2017
by arrangement with Aram Publishing
English text edited by Scott Forbes
English edition © big & SMALL 2017

Distributed in the United States and Canada by
Lerner Publishing Group, Inc.
241 First Avenue North
Minneapolis, MN 55401 U.S.A.
www.lernerbooks.com

Photo credits:
Page 28, top: © AStrangerintheAlps; bottom: © Tim Evanson
Page 29, top: © Haplochromis; center: © FunkMonk;
bottom: © Clément Bardot

ISBN: 978-1-925235-19-7
Printed in Korea

To learn more about dinosaur fossils, see page 28.
For information on the main groups of dinosaurs,
see the Dinosaur Family Tree on page 30.

Alioramus
on the Hunt

Alioramus

big & SMALL

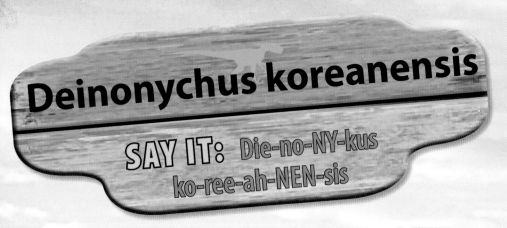

Deinonychus koreanensis

SAY IT: Die-no-NY-kus
ko-ree-ah-NEN-sis

Roaring and snarling, the Deinonychus koreanensis
attacked the Koreaceratops as it bent down to the
water to drink. Before it could do anything, the
Deinonychus were all over it, biting and ripping
at it with their terrifying hooked talons.

Deinonychus koreanensis was related to the North American Deinonychus. Like its American cousin, it was small but ferocious. Groups, or packs, of Deinonychus would surround and attack prey, including larger dinosaurs.

LENGTH: 13 feet (4 meters)

HEIGHT: 4 feet (1.2 meters)

WEIGHT: 175 pounds (80 kilograms)

WHEN IT LIVED: TRIASSIC JURASSIC **CRETACEOUS**

GROUP: Theropods

DIET: Meat

WHERE IT LIVED: Asia (South Korea)

After struggling for a while, the Koreaceratops fell to the ground. The Deinonychus koreanensis gathered round and began tearing at its flesh. This meal would keep them satisfied for quite some time.

KOREACERATOPS

GROUP: Ceratopsians
DIET: Plants
WHEN IT LIVED: Early Cretaceous
WHERE IT LIVED: Asia
(South Korea)
LENGTH: 7.5 feet (2.3 meters)
HEIGHT: 2 feet (0.6 meters)
WEIGHT: 330 pounds
(150 kilograms)

Deinonychus means "terrible claw."
All Deinonychus had an especially long,
curved claw on each foot, measuring up
to 4 inches (10 centimeters) in length.
This was its most dangerous weapon.

9

Segnosaurus

SAY IT:
Seh-nyo-SAW-rus

The Segnosaurus were busy
digging a hole in which to lay eggs.
They got a fright when a Gigantoraptor
suddenly appeared behind them.
The Segnosaurus made a fierce noise
and raised their long claws. The
Gigantoraptor then backed away.

When Segnosaurus was discovered, scientists found it puzzling. It had a long neck like the long-necked sauropod dinosaurs; a strong beak like that of the ostrich-like dinosaurs; and sharp claws like those of a meat-eater. Eventually they decided it belonged to the therizinosaurs, a group of large bird-like dinosaurs with long claws.

GIGANTORAPTOR

GROUP: Theropods
DIET: Meat and plants
WHEN IT LIVED: Late Cretaceous
WHERE IT LIVED: Asia (China, Mongolia)
LENGTH: 36 feet (11 meters)
HEIGHT: 16 feet (5 meters)
WEIGHT: 2.2 tons
(2 tonnes)

The Segnosaurus went down to the river. Some Bactrosaurus were feeding on plants there. The Segnosaurus waded into the river, stood still, and waited patiently. As a big fish swam past, one of the Segnosaurus thrust its claws into the water and snatched it up. Then it popped the fish into its mouth and swallowed it whole. Yum!

BACTROSAURUS

GROUP: Ornithopods
DIET: Plants
WHEN IT LIVED: Late Cretaceous
WHERE IT LIVED: Asia (China)
LENGTH: 13–20 feet (4–6 meters)
HEIGHT: 6.6 feet (2 meters)
WEIGHT: 1.2–1.7 tons
(1–1.5 tonnes)

HEIGHT: 6.6 feet (2 meters)
LENGTH: 21.5 feet (6.5 meters)
WEIGHT: 880 pounds (400 kilograms)

WHEN IT LIVED: **TRIASSIC** JURASSIC CRETACEOUS
GROUP: **Theropods**   DIET: **Meat and plants**
WHERE IT LIVED: **Asia** (China, Mongolia)

12

As well as for catching fish, Segnosaurus used its long claws to pull down high branches and to dig into insect nests.

Montanoceratops

SAY IT:
Mon-ta-noh-SER-ah-tops

A female Montanoceratops was taking her baby on its first walk away from its nest. The baby kept trying to eat every plant it came across. But some tasted horrible!

The mother had to steer the baby toward plants she knew would taste nice and be good for her. She would soon learn!

Montanoceratops was related to big horned dinosaurs like Triceratops. But it was much smaller and, although it had a similar neck frill and a parrot-like beak, it did not have horns.

Montanoceratops used its strong beak to rip up tough, low-growing plants. It had teeth in its upper jaw for chopping the plants up further.

HEIGHT: **3.3 feet (1 meter)**

LENGTH: **10 feet (3 meters)**

WEIGHT: **880 pounds (400 kilograms)**

WHEN IT LIVED: | **TRIASSIC** | **JURASSIC** | **CRETACEOUS**

GROUP: **Ceratopsians**

DIET: **Plants**

WHERE IT LIVED: **North America (USA)**

Megaraptor

SAY IT:
Meg-ah-RAP-tor

The Megaraptors had been hunting all day and had caught little. Finally, they came across a group of small plant-eating dinosaurs and began chasing them through the forest. Soon they had one cornered. They were just about to pounce on it when, all of a sudden, a Giganotosaurus leaped out of the trees and grabbed their prey.

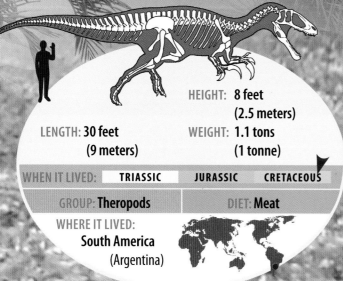

LENGTH: **30 feet**
(**9 meters**)

HEIGHT: **8 feet**
(**2.5 meters**)

WEIGHT: **1.1 tons**
(**1 tonne**)

WHEN IT LIVED:	TRIASSIC	JURASSIC	CRETACEOUS

GROUP: **Theropods**	DIET: **Meat**

WHERE IT LIVED:
South America
(Argentina)

The Megaraptors weren't going to stand for that! Even though the Giganotosaurus was enormous, they leaped onto it and started biting and tearing at it.

The Giganotosaurus fought back fiercely. It was injured and bleeding badly, but eventually it managed to shake the Megaraptors off and escape into the safety of the forest.

Megaraptor had one especially long claw on the first finger of each hand. It was up to 12 inches (30 centimeters) long.

Megaraptor means "giant thief." This dinosaur was a terrifying hunter. It was big, could run fast, and had long, hooked, sharp claws. It was also intelligent. Groups, or packs, of Megaraptors worked together to hunt and trap prey.

GIGANOTOSAURUS

GROUP: Theropods
DIET: Meat
WHEN IT LIVED: Late Cretaceous
WHERE IT LIVED: South America (Argentina)
LENGTH: 40–46 feet (12–14 meters)
HEIGHT: 23–26 feet (7–8 meters)
WEIGHT: 6.6–7.7 tons
(6–7 tonnes)

Plateosaurus

SAY IT:
Pla-tay-oh-SAW-rus

Two Plateosaurus were exploring a new forest. They examined the low-growing plants on the ground and found some particularly tasty shoots. Then they reached up high into the trees and nibbled on some delicious leaves. They were very happy to have found this place!

Plateosaurus means "broad lizard." The name refers to its wide, flat teeth. Plateosaurus used these like a saw to cut through plants.

Plateosaurus lived early in the age of the dinosaurs and was one of the first large plant-eaters. It wasn't as big as many of the later long-necked dinosaurs, but it was still the biggest dinosaur of its time.

Plateosaurus walked on all four legs. However, to reach
high into the trees, it could rise up on its back legs,
using its tail to help it balance, and stretch its neck
upward. Plateosaurus had sharp front claws,
which helped it grab and snap off plants and
dig roots out of the ground.

LENGTH: **26 feet**
(8 meters)

HEIGHT: **10–13 feet**
(3–4 meters)

WEIGHT: **3.3 tons**
(3 tonnes)

WHEN IT LIVED: **TRIASSIC** JURASSIC CRETACEOUS

GROUP: **Sauropods**

DIET: **Plants**

WHERE IT LIVED:
Europe (Germany,
France, Switzerland)

Alioramus

SAY IT:
Ah-lee-oh-RAH-mus

The male Alioramus puffed up its chest and thrust its head toward a female Alioramus. It was showing off the crest on its snout. Only the male Alioramus had a crest.

The female Alioramus looked at the male uncertainly, then turned her back on him and walked off. Clearly, she was not impressed!

Alioramus is related to Tyrannosaurus. Its name means "different branch." It was the crest on Alioramus' snout that made scientists realize that it was not just a small Tyrannosaurus but a new kind of dinosaur.

As the female Alioramus was walking away, the male spotted a Tsintaosaurus. It charged after it, and brought it to the ground. The female Alioramus rushed over and joined in the attack. Soon the two of them were enjoying a feast.

LENGTH: 20 feet
(6 meters)

HEIGHT: 6.6 feet
(2 meters)

WEIGHT: 1500 pounds
(700 kilograms)

WHEN IT LIVED: TRIASSIC   JURASSIC   CRETACEOUS

GROUP: Theropods

DIET: Meat

WHERE IT LIVED:
Asia (Mongolia)

Alioramus was not as big as some other meat-eaters of the same period, such as Tarbosaurus, and it had a fairly weak bite. So it often hunted in groups, or packs. Often, packs of Alioramus hid among trees and ambushed prey as they passed by.

TSINTAOSAURUS

GROUP: Ornithopods
DIET: Plants
WHEN IT LIVED: Late Cretaceous
WHERE IT LIVED: Asia (China, South Korea)
LENGTH: 30–33 feet (9–10 meters)
HEIGHT: 13 feet (4 meters)
WEIGHT: 3.3–4.4 tons
(3–4 tonnes)

Dinosaur Fossils

Fossils are the remains of dinosaurs. They can be hard parts of dinosaurs, such as bones and teeth, that have slowly turned to stone. Or they may be impressions of bones, teeth, or skin preserved in rocks.

▲ Model of a Deinonychus koreanensis skeleton

Deinonychus koreanensis

Fossils of Deinonychus koreanensis, including a leg bone, claw, and teeth, were first found by Professor Kim Hang Mook in South Korea in 1979. Initially, it seemed that the fossils came from a previously unknown type of dinosaur and it was given the name "Koreanosaurus," in honor of where it had been discovered. However, in 1993, scientists decided that the dinosaur was actually a new type of Deinonychus and its name was changed to Deinonychus koreanensis.

Segnosaurus

In 1973, an expedition organized by the Soviet Union and Mongolia discovered the first Segnosaurus fossils in Mongolia. Others were found there in 1974 and 1975, and in 1979 Mongolian dinosaur expert Altangerel Perle called the dinosaur Segnosaurus. The name means "slow lizard" and is a reference to its big, thick legs, which suggest it wouldn't have been able to run very fast.

▲ Model of a Segnosaurus nest

▲ Model of a Montanoceratops fossil

Montanoceratops

Fossils of Montanoceratops were first found by dinosaur hunter Barnum Brown in 1916, in Montana, USA. Scientists decided the fossils were of a dinosaur called Leptoceratops. But in 1951 dinosaur expert Charles Sternberg pointed out that the Montana fossils were not the same as Leptoceratops and had to be a different dinosaur. It was named Montanoceratops, which means "Montana horned face."

Megaraptor

In the Patagonian region of Argentina, in South America, dinosaur expert Fernando Novas found a fossilized leg bone and a claw that was an incredible 14 inches (35 centimeters) long. At first scientists thought this must be part of a hind foot, but once more Megaraptor bones were found they realized it was a front claw.

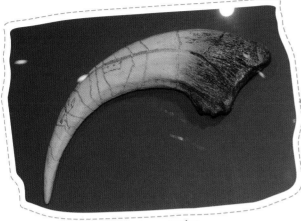

▲ Megaraptor claw

Plateosaurus

A German doctor, Johann Engelhardt, found the first Plateosaurus fossils in Bavaria, Germany, in 1837, and the dinosaur was given its name three years later. Dozens of Plateosaurus fossils have since been discovered all over Europe, including in Germany, France, and Switzerland. Large groups of fossils have been found in one place, suggesting that Plateosaurus liked living in large herds.

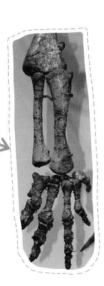

◄ Front claw of a Plateosaurus

Alioramus

In early 1970, a combined Soviet Union–Mongolian expedition to Mongolia's Gobi Desert located a skull, leg bone, backbone, and hipbone from the same dinosaur. In 1976, Russian dinosaur expert Sergei Kurzanov studied the fossils and decided they came from a relative of Tyrannosaurus. However, he pointed out that it was very different from most other Tyrannosaurs, and he gave it the name Alioramus, meaning "different branch."

▲ Model of an Alioramus skull

201 MILLION YEARS AGO

THE DINOSAUR FAMILY TREE

Carnosaurs (large meat-eate

Coelurosaurs (small meat-eaters

Theropods (meat-eaters)

Saurischians (lizard-hipped dinosaurs)

Plateosaurus

Sauropods (long-necked plant-eaters)

Therizinosaurs (long-clawed dinosaurs)

Stegosaurs (plate-backed plant-eaters)

Dinosaur ancestors

Ankylosaurs (armored plant-eaters)

Ornithischians (bird-hipped dinosaurs)

Ornithopods (two-legged plant-eaters)

Dinosaurs lived on Earth from about 245 million years ago until about 66 million years ago — long before the first humans. After the first dinosaurs appeared, they spread to all the continents and many different kinds of dinosaurs emerged. This chart shows the main groups of dinosaurs.

Pterosaurs (flying reptiles)

Ichthyosaurs (marine reptiles)

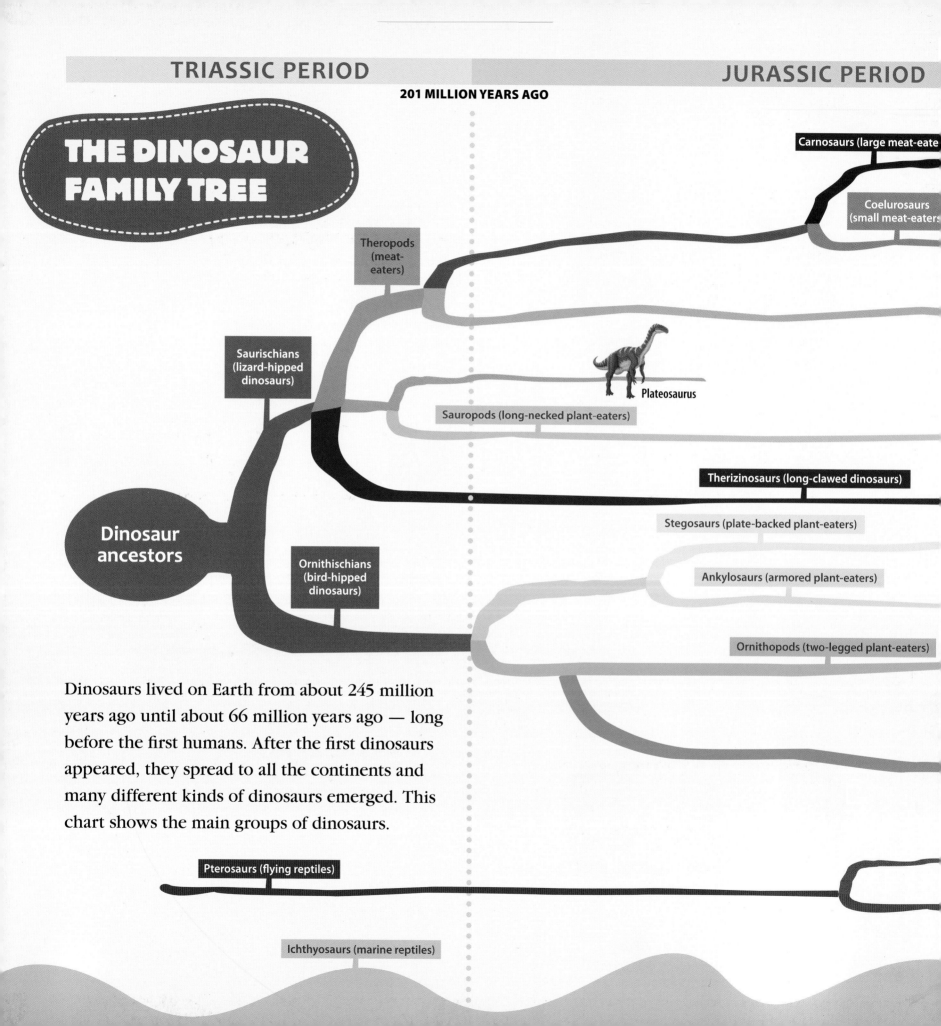